TERMITES

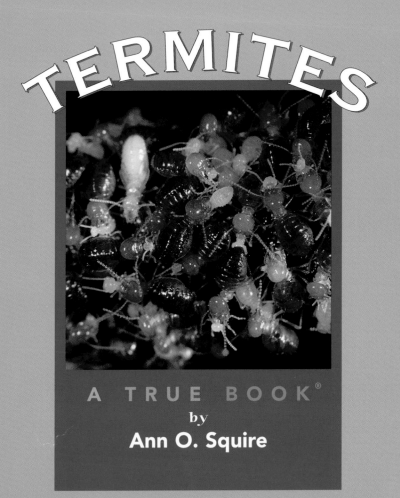

A TRUE BOOK®

by
Ann O. Squire

Children's Press®
A Division of Scholastic Inc.

New York Toronto London Auckland Sydney
Mexico City New Delhi Hong Kong
Danbury, Connecticut

Ants confront a
termite soldier.

Reading Consultant
Nanci R. Vargus, Ed.D.
Assistant Professor
Literacy Education
University of Indianapolis
Indianapolis, IN

Content Consultant
Jeff Hahn
Department of Entomology
University of Minnesota

The photograph on the cover
shows a soldier termite. The
photograph on the title page
shows a termite swarm.

Dedication:
For Evan

Library of Congress Cataloging-in-Publication Data

Squire, Ann.
   Termites / by Ann O. Squire
      p. cm. — (True books)
   Includes bibliographical references and index (p.   ).
   ISBN 0-516-22660-6 (lib. bdg.)   0-516-29360-5 (pbk.)
   1. Termites—Juvenile literature. [1. Termites.] I. Title. II. True book.
QL529.S76 2003
595.7'36—dc21

                                                      2002005894

1 2 3 4 5 6 7 8 9 10 R 12 11 10 09 08 07 06 05 04 03

Contents

Many termites look like little white ants.

What Is a Termite?

Have you ever heard someone talk about "white ants," or seen an insect that looked like an ant with a light-colored body? Chances are you were looking at a termite. Similar to ants, termites are insects with three body segments and strong, biting **mouthparts**.

5

And like ants, termites are very social. They live and work in large, complex colonies. But that's where the similarity ends. Although they look like ants, and act a bit like ants, termites are actually close relatives of cockroaches.

Scientists believe that termites evolved from their cockroach ancestors about 150 million years ago. They haven't changed much in all those years and are considered to be primitive insects.

Scientists think that termites evolved from the cockroach family.

But as you'll learn later in this book, termite social behavior is not primitive at all.

Termites have pale, soft bodies that are always in danger of drying out. To prevent this, they spend most of their time underground, where it is cool and damp. Termites will do almost anything to avoid the outside world. They even build covered mud tunnels called shelter tubes. These tubes protect them while they travel from their nest to a source of food.

Because they spend their lives in the dark, vision is not very important to most termites.

Termites build shelter tubes so they can travel safely from place to place.

In fact, many termites do not even have eyes! The exceptions are winged reproductive termites, which need to see

Many termites live underground and do not need eyes in their dark world.

where they are going when they fly.

Instead of visual cues, termites use chemical signals to communicate with one another. Every termite colony has its own special chemical "odor." If an intruder enters the nest, the termites can tell right away

because the nest has a different smell. When this happens,
the termites release an alarm
pheromone that lets the
soldier termites know it's time
to attack. Termites also use
pheromones to tell one another
about new food sources.

Termites use chemical signals to stay in touch with one another.

Eat and Be Eaten

Termites can do something that almost no other animal in the world can do: they can eat wood. Some eat dry wood, while others prefer damp, rotten wood. Dead trees, rotting fences, telephone poles, and the beams holding up your house are all on the menu for

Termites are the only insects that can eat wood.

wood-eating termites. How are termites able to digest wood while other animals can't? The amazing answer is that termites can't digest wood by themselves either. They depend on tiny

13

bacteria and **protozoans** (single-celled organisms) in their intestines to do it for them. Without these helpful **microorganisms**, the termites would starve to death no matter how much wood they ate.

When young termites first hatch from their eggs, they do not have these micro-organisms and cannot digest wood. But the adult termites quickly solve that problem by giving the youngsters a first

Young termites need to get special bacteria and protozoans from adults before they can digest wood.

meal that contains the necessary bacteria and protozoans. From then on, they can digest wood with no difficulty at all.

These worker termites are storing grass in elephant dung.

Not all termites eat wood. Some species eat dead grasses, plants, leaf litter, and dung. There are even termites that eat mushrooms, which they grow in special gardens inside their nests. In the same way that humans keep cows, one type of termite shares its nest with small beetles. These beetles secrete a fluid the termites love to drink.

We may think of termites as pests, but they actually play an important role in recycling dead wood and enriching the soil. They also help to provide food for other animals. Most animals cannot eat wood, but they can eat termites.

A monitor lizard breaks into a termite mound to look for a meal.

So without knowing it, termites are turning wood into something that can be used by millions of other animals. In the tropics, termites are the favorite food of many reptiles, birds, and mammals, including some humans.

Termites and the Temperature

Have you ever heard of global warming? Scientists believe that a buildup of gases in Earth's atmosphere is causing our climate to get warmer every year. Most of these harmful gases come from burning coal and other fuels. But a surprisingly large amount comes from termites, which produce a gas called methane as they digest wood. So if your weather is feeling hotter, termites may be partly to blame!

Termites carry bits of wood home to eat.

Termites eating an old stump

The Termite Colony

Like ants, termites live in colonies made up of thousands, or even millions, of individuals that all work together to keep the society running smoothly. However, termite colonies are very different from ant colonies. Unlike an ant colony, which has only one queen, a termite

A termite queen lays eggs for the colony (above). This queen nymph is a daughter of the royal pair (right).

colony has both a king and queen. These termites found the colony and stay together for life. Every termite in the colony is either a son or daughter of this royal pair, so the colony is one huge family. Some biologists think that termite colonies are the most sophisticated families ever to evolve on Earth.

There are three different groups of termites, called **castes**, in a typical colony. The reproductive caste includes the king and queen. These two termites produce most of the young. The reproductive caste also includes other male

Members of the reproductive caste have well-developed wings.

and female termites that usually do not reproduce. If anything should happen to the king or queen, these "backup" termites are ready to step in and take over the job of reproduction for the colony. Members of the reproductive caste usually have well-developed eyes and wings.

Members of the two remaining castes, the soldiers and the workers, do most of the work for the colony. Soldier termites with large **mandibles**, or jaws, and armored heads have the job of protecting the colony. Worker termites are small, wingless, and usually blind. They concentrate on enlarging

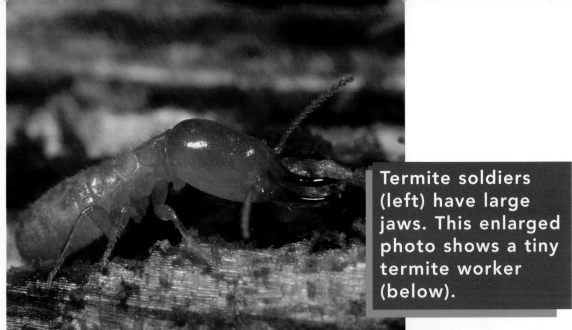

Termite soldiers (left) have large jaws. This enlarged photo shows a tiny termite worker (below).

and cleaning the nest, caring for the young, and keeping the colony supplied with food.

Nymphs can sense the pheromones in the colony as the grown termites groom each other.

Termites have a fascinating way of keeping their numbers in balance. Each caste produces its own special pheromones. These chemicals are passed around as the termites lick and groom each other, and as they clean the developing eggs and **nymphs** (young termites). If there are too many soldier termites, for example, the level of "soldier" pheromone in the colony is very high. When this happens, few eggs and nymphs develop into soldiers. But if many soldiers have been killed defending the colony, low levels of "soldier" pheromone cause many more eggs and nymphs to grow up to be soldiers.

Termite Homes

Termites eat wood, but only a few actually live in wood. Wood-inhabiting termites find a dead branch or log, eat their way inside, and then live in the tunnels they have created. The problem is that, sooner or later, the termites eat up their home. With no food left, the colony dies.

These wood-inhabiting termites live in an old tree stump.

Subterranean termites
live below the soil.

Other termite species have
solved this problem by living
underground. They go outside
the nest to search for wood to

eat. Because ground-nesting termites can find food in many different places, their colonies become much larger than those of wood-inhabiting termites. Some subterranean (underground) termite cities are home to several million residents.

While most termites live in nests underground, some species prefer high-rise homes. In Africa, it is not uncommon to see towering brown mounds

of soil. These mounds, called **termitaries**, are created by the termites that live inside.

Some termite mounds can reach 20 feet (6 meters) in height and can weigh several tons. No matter how large it eventually becomes, every termite mound starts out as a tiny underground chamber excavated by the king and queen. As their eggs hatch and the colony grows, the termites expand their home by tunneling below and building above the ground. To construct the tower, termite workers carry small bits of soil to the top of the nest. After mixing the soil with a few drops of saliva, they push the cement-like mixture into place. When dry, the walls of the termite mound are as hard as rock.

As the termites build the mound, they are careful to excavate tunnels leading from the bottom up to an "attic" space at the top of the tower. These ventilation tunnels keep fresh air flowing through the termitary. Without this built-in

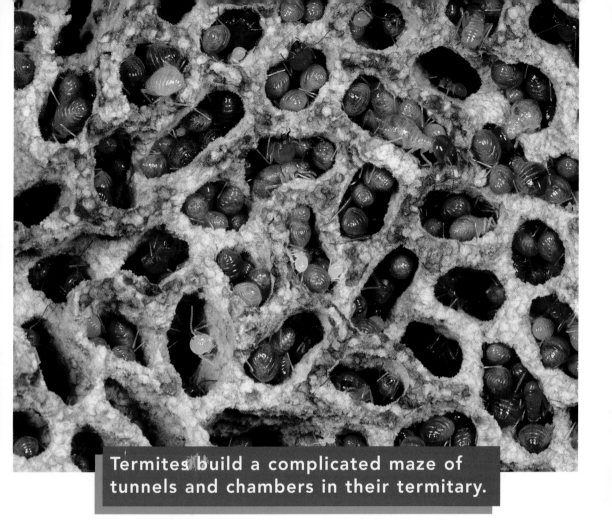

Termites build a complicated maze of
tunnels and chambers in their termitary.

air-conditioning system, the
termites inside would quickly
overheat and die in the searing
heat of the African plains.

Termite Enemies and Defenses

Termites have many enemies, including birds, reptiles, mammals, and even other insects. One of the biggest threats is a marauding anteater, which uses its razor-sharp claws to rip open the nest. Then it uses its long tongue to lick up

An anteater is raiding a termite nest in Central America.

scurrying termites. Once their nest is damaged, the termites often fall victim to an even more dangerous predator: a swarm of ants.

Ants are very dangerous enemies to termites.

Ants are considered to be the termite's deadliest enemy because they raid termite nests so often. Though it is usually a losing battle, termites do have a wide variety of strategies that they use against intruding ants. Since an ant attack is always a possibility, many termite workers never leave the nest without bringing soldiers along for protection. With their bodyguards by their sides, the workers can travel farther from the nest in search of food.

A group of ants carries away their termite prey.

If the group does encounter an army of ants, the termite soldiers have some impressive weapons to defend themselves and the other termites. Some soldiers have long snouts through which they spray poisonous chemicals or sticky glue at their attackers. Others use several defenses at once. First they use their powerful mandibles to bite the enemy and then coat the wound with poison.

A termite soldier sprays chemicals at its attacker.

Some termite soldiers have very large heads that they use to block off entrances to their nests when enemies attack.

And what if ants attack while the termites are inside their nest? For some termite species, this is a chance to avoid conflict altogether. Soldiers of these species are equipped with large, blunt heads that they use to plug up the entrances to the nest, leaving their would-be attackers out in the cold.

To Find Out More

Here are some additional resources to help you learn more about termites:

 **Books**

Brimner, Larry Dane. **Cockroaches** (True Books). Danbury, CT: Children's Press, 1999.

Green, Jen. **Insect Societies** (Nature Watch). New York, NY: Lorenz Books, 2002.

Pascoe, Elaine. **Ants** (Nature Close-Up). Woodbridge, CT: Blackbirch Press, 1998.

Robinson, W. Wright. **Animal Architects: How Insects Build Their Amazing Homes.** Woodbridge, CT: Blackbirch Press, 1999.

Organizations and Online Sites

Insecta Inspecta
http://www.insecta-inspecta.com/termites/macrotermes/index.html

This site contains information about and photos of African mound-building termites.

University of Toronto
http://www.utoronto.ca/forest/termite/termite.htm

This Web site from the Urban Entomology Program at the University of Toronto has information on everything you might want to know about termites, including species lists, photos, movies, and links to other termite Web sites.

Important Words

bacteria single-celled organisms that live in soil, water, organic matter, or the bodies of plants and animals

caste a group of termites that performs a particular function in the colony

mandibles jaws

microorganisms organisms that are microscopic in size, such as bacteria

mouthparts structures near the mouth of an insect that are adapted for gathering or eating food

nymph an immature termite

pheromone a chemical substance produced by an animal that serves as a signal to other animals of the same species

protozoans single-celled organisms that are found in almost every habitat

termitary a termite nest or mound

Index

Meet the Author

Ann O. Squire has a Ph.D. in animal behavior. Before becoming a writer, she spent several years studying African electric fish and the special signals they use to communicate with each other. Dr. Squire is the author of many books on animals and natural science topics, including *Beetles, Crickets and Grasshoppers, Seashells,* and *Rocks and Minerals.* She lives with her children, Evan and Emma, in Katonah, New York.